The GAMBOLS

by Dobs + Barry Appleby

BOOK No 17

A COLLECTION OF CARTOONS OF THE FAMOUS CHARACTERS FROM THE DAILY EXPRESS AND THE SUNDAY EXPRESS

FOR VARIOUS REASONS MANY OF THESE CARTOONS ARE PUBLISHED HERE FOR THE FIRST TIME

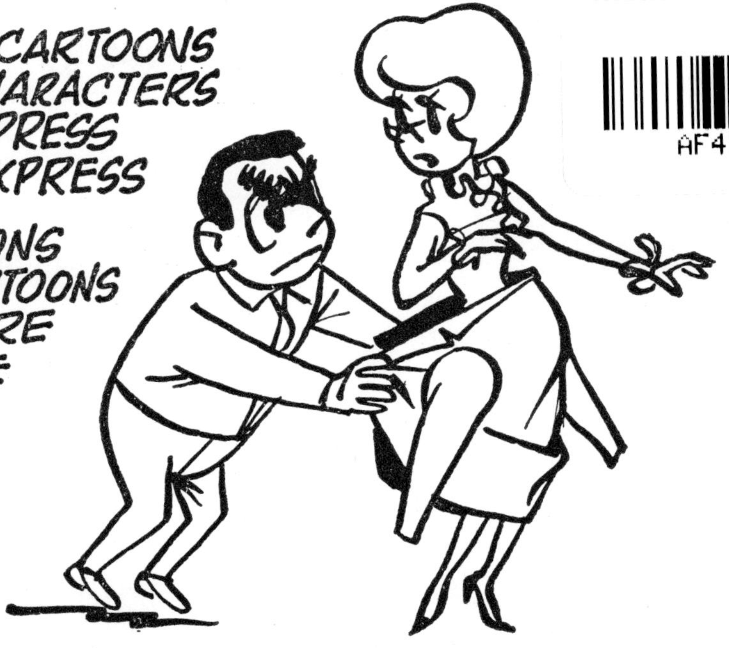

4/-

WHAT LOVELY HAIR THAT GIRL HAS
IT'S A PIECE

HUH?
A WIG YOU STUPID

OH..... POOR GIRL
18-5

MILLY'S HUSBAND ALWAYS CHANGES FOR DINNER
©1968
Dobs + Barry Appleby

AS SOON AS HE GETS HOME IN THE EVENING HE CHANGES

WELL, I'LL CHANGE IN THE EVENING IF IT'LL MAKE YOU HAPPY

THAT'S NOT WHAT I MEANT
26-3

YES, WE'D LOVE TO COME.. BUT I'D BETTER ASK GEORGE FIRST
©1968 Dobs + Barry Appleby

GEORGE SAYS HE'D BE DELIGHTED

HURRY UP DEAR— WE'RE GOING OUT
20-3

YOU DID WHAT?
I BOUGHT IT AT AN AUCTION SALE
©1967 Dobs + Barry Appleby

WHY?
I THOUGHT YOU'D LIKE IT

WELL, I CAN'T MAKE UP MY MIND WHETHER YOU'RE JUST PLAIN STUPID

OR TRYING TO BE FUNNY
LOT 7
2-11

WHERE DID YOU BUY THAT?
FROM A DOOR-TO-DOOR SALESMAN
©1968 Dos+
Barry Appleby

BUT THAT'S THE THIRD THING YOU'VE BOUGHT AT THE DOOR THIS WEEK
HE'S SO PERSUASIVE

YOU'D BETTER SEE HIM THE NEXT TIME HE CALLS
RIGHT!

I'LL BE READY FOR HIM
TAR
BEST FEATHERS
29-5

LOCKED!
©1968 Dos+
Barry Appleby

WHY DID YOU LOCK THE BACK DOOR?
WAX POLISH
17-2

WE DEMAND SHORTER HOURS
STRIKE NOW
©1967
Dobs + Barry Appleby

THAT'S A WONDERFUL IDEA
STRIKE NOW
WE DEMAND SHORTER HOURS

I HAVE SO MANY JOBS PILING UP AT HOME FOR YOU TO DO

STRIKE NOW
I DEMAND LONGER HOURS AT WORK
20-9

IF THEY HAD A BETTER MAN TO LEAD THE ATTACK
©1967
Dobs + Barry Appleby

AND KEPT TWO MEN BACK IN DEFENCE...
TOOLS

TAKE NO NOTICE OF GAYE

IT'S JUST HER WAY OF HINTING
PAINT
28-10

ON SAFARI
THE MOST EXCITING THING THAT HAPPENED TO US DURING THE YEAR WAS OUR VISIT TO THE GAME RESERVES IN SOUTH AFRICA. WHILE WE WERE THERE WE DID SOME CARTOONS WHICH APPEARED IN THE SOUTH AFRICAN NEWSPAPERS. THE FOLLOWING PAGES GIVE YOU SOME IDEA OF LIFE ON SAFARI

WELL, WE'D BETTER START PACKING IF WE'RE GOING TO THE GAME RESERVE TOMORROW
© 1968 Dobs + Barry Appleby

SUN HAT... A SPARE SHIRT I SUPPOSE.. SOCKS .. BOOTS... SLIPPERS FOR THE REST CAMP.. RAZOR.. TORCH

PYJAMAS.. NO, I'LL SLEEP IN MY UNDERPANTS ... MUST KEEP THE LUGGAGE LIGHT

ER.. GAYE DEAR.... ARE WE GOING TO THE SAME PLACE ?
MAKE-UP
SUN SUITS
BIKINI
COCKTAIL DRESSES
1

MOVIE CAMERA ?
YES
STILL CAMERA ?
© 1968 Dobs + Barry Appleby

TELESCOPIC LENS – ZOOM LENS – CLOSE UP LENS – FILMS ?

TRIPOD – LENS HOOD – FILTERS – EXPOSURE METER ?
YES

RIGHT – COME ON THEN
GAME RESERVE
2

DON'T WORRY DEAR

THAT FENCE IS QUITE STRONG

NEVERTHELESS I'D SLEEP BETTER IF IT WERE A MOAT

NOW DON'T FORGET WHEN WE COME FACE TO FACE WITH THE LION STOP THE CAR

AND REMAIN QUITE STILL WHILE I FILM IT

HAVE WE GOT EVERYTHING WE NEED?

EVERYTHING EXCEPT THE NERVE TONIC

...AND NOW YOU ARE IN THE HOME OF THE WILDEST AND FIERCEST LIONS IN AFRICA
GUIDE

MAY WE REMIND YOU NOT TO LEAVE YOUR CAR
GUIDE

SLAM
5

ISN'T HE SWEET— I DO LIKE HIM

THE POINT IS DEAR DOES HE LIKE YOU
6

DID YOU EVER HAVE A DAY LIKE THIS?

NOT VOLUNTARILY
© 1968 Bobs + Barry Appleby
7

SWITCH OFF THE ENGINE, DEAR
© 1968 Bobs + Barry Appleby

AND LET THE CAR GLIDE DOWN THIS LITTLE HILL

THIS IS WHAT I LIKE BEST ABOUT THE GAME RESERVE

IT'S ALL SO QUIET AND PEACEFUL
8

EEK!
©1968
Dobs+
Barry Appleby

GEORGE

I TOLD YOU NOT TO GET OUT OF THE CAR

WELL, TELL ME AGAIN HOW MUCH I'M ENJOYING MYSELF— I KEEP FORGETTING
9

EEK
©1968
Dobs+Barry Appleby

WHAT'S THE MATTER ?

SOMETHING MADE A NOISE IN THE GRASS
OH ...

I THOUGHT IT WAS YOU BREAKING THE SOUND BARRIER
10

'BYE 'BYE
©1968 Dobs + Barry Appleby

IT'S BEEN NICE SEEING YOU MADAM

WHY DID YOU CALL THAT HIPPO 'MADAM'?

BECAUSE IT REMINDED ME OF THE PRESIDENT OF OUR WOMAN'S CLUB
11

©1968 Dobs + Barry Appleby

WE'LL HAVE TO TRY AND GET IT DOWN WITH A STICK

THERE'S NEVER A GIRAFFE ABOUT WHEN YOU NEED ONE
12

READERS OFTEN ASK HOW FLIVVER GOT HIS NAME — WELL
HERE IS THE EXPLANATION ONCE MORE. BEFORE HE WAS
BORN HIS PARENTS WERE SAVING UP TO BUY AN OLD CAR —
A REAL OLD FLIVVER IN FACT. BUT WHEN THEY DISCOVERED
THAT THEY WERE ABOUT TO BECOME PARENTS THEY
DECIDED THAT THEY COULDN'T AFFORD A CAR AFTER ALL
— SO THE BABY WAS GIVEN THE NAME FLIVVER

AH! THAT'S GEORGE WITH THE CHILDREN
RINGG
©1967 Dobs + Barry Appleby

I EXPECT THEY'LL HAVE GROWN

EEK!

29-12

LET'S SURPRISE AUNTIE AND COOK BREAKFAST
WHAT SHALL WE COOK?
©1968 Dobs + Barry Appleby

SCRAMBLED EGGS
HOW DO YOU DO THAT?
COOK BOOK

WELL, IT SAYS HERE "BREAK TWO EGGS INTO A BOWL"
AND HOW DO YOU DO THAT?
COOK BOOK

EASY
EGGS
29-4

CAN I HAVE SOME MONEY FOR AN ICE?
©1968 Dobs + Barry Appleby

NO - MONEY DOESN'T GROW ON TREES

YOU MUST LEARN TO EARN YOUR MONEY

HOW MUCH IS IT WORTH NOT TO TAKE THE LID OFF MY MOUSE'S BOX?
30-4

DOESN'T SHE LOOK SWEET
©1968 Dobs + Barry Appleby

CAN I MAKE YOU SOME TEA AUNTIE?

NO, NO, AUNTIE, LET US WASH THE DISHES

I WONDER WHAT THEY'VE BEEN UP TO NOW?
1-5

WHO GAVE YOU ALL THAT MONEY?
©1968 Dobs + Barry Appleby

AUNTIE GAYE

WHAT FOR?

FOR GOING THE WHOLE AFTERNOON WITHOUT BREAKING ANYTHING
22-4

TAKE IT OUT OF HERE
©1968 Dobs + Barry Appleby

HE WON'T BE ANY BOTHER — I'LL KEEP HIM IN MY BEDROOM

OUT.. OUT.. OUT

BUT HE MIGHT CHANGE INTO A HANDSOME PRINCE
23-4

NO MORE — YOU'VE EATEN ALL THE CAKES AND ALL THE APPLES
CAKE
©1968 Dobs + Barry Appleby

AND HAD FOUR ICES EACH
CAKE

WE'RE NOT GETTING ANYWHERE STAYING HERE

LET'S GO OVER TO YOUR HOUSE
26-4

I'LL RUN THE BABY-SITTER HOME IN THE CAR
SHOOH, DEAR
©1968 Dobs + Barry Appleby

YOU'LL WAKE THE CHILDREN

WHERE'S THE BABY-SITTER?

GONE TO SEE HER LAWYER
19-4

MONDAY & TUESDAY
COME ON LAZY BONES — IT'S PAST EIGHT O'CLOCK
©1968 Dobs + Barry Appleby

WEDNESDAY & THURSDAY
FLIVVER! MIGGY! — YOUR BREAKFAST'S GETTING COLD

FRIDAY
MIGGY — IT'S NEARLY NINE O'CLOCK

SATURDAY & SUNDAY
BUT IT'S GONE SIX O'CLOCK
20-4

WHERE DID YOU GET ALL THOSE SNACKS?
THEY'RE LEFT-OVERS FROM AUNTIE'S BRIDGE PARTY
©1968 Dobs + Barry Appleby

HOW DID YOU GET SO MANY?
EASY

TOLD THEM I DIDN'T FANCY THEM

SAID THAT I'D WATCHED AUNTIE GAYE MAKE THEM
10-1

DID YOU ENJOY YOUR FISHING TRIP?
SUPER
FAB
©1968 Bob & Barry Appleby

CATCH MANY FISH?
NO

UNCLE GEORGE FRIGHTENED THEM ALL AWAY
OH? HOW?

WHEN HE FELL IN
13/4

TRY THE ONE IN THE HIGH STREET
©1968 Bob & Barry Appleby

NO?... WELL THANK YOU ANYWAY

HE WON'T TAKE HER EITHER

WELL, THERE MUST BE A DENTIST SOMEWHERE THAT SHE HASN'T BITTEN
TELEPHONE DIRECTORY
15-1

IT'S TIME FOR BED
©1968
Dobs+Barry Appleby

NO MORE QUESTIONS

NO, NOT ANOTHER SINGLE QUESTION OF ANY SORT— OFF TO BED

GEORGE, DEAR, JUST WHY DOES AN AIRPLANE MAKE A BANG WHEN IT GOES THROUGH THE SOUND BARRIER?
8-1

©1968 Dobs+Barry Appleby

I WONDER WHAT IT'S LIKE TO HAVE A HOT BATH
11-1

CRY-LOUDER-THAT'S IT-NOW GO AND GIVE HIM ALL THAT JAZZ ABOUT NEEDING MORE POCKET MONEY
©1968
Bobs+Barry Appleby

OH, VERY WELL HERE YOU ARE

AND TEN PER CENT FOR ME
HUH?

I'M HER AGENT
3-1

FIVE...FOUR ...THREE
©1968
Bobs+Barry Appleby

TWO...ONE

BLAST OFF!

12-1

WHEN THE BREATHALYSER CAST IT'S GLOOM ON PARTIES GEORGE THOUGHT UP A SCHEME TO SOLVE THE UNIVERSAL PARTY PROBLEM. HIS IDEA IS THAT THE WINNER OF A NIGHT'S GAME HAS TO STAY 'DRY' AT THE NEXT PARTY AND ACT AS CHAUFFEUR TO THE OTHER PLAYERS.

I ONLY ASKED YOU IF THAT WAS THE FIRST TIME YOU'D EVER HAD FOUR ACES IN ONE HAND
©1968 Dobs + Barry Appleby
5-7

CARD TABLE... CHIPS... A NEW PACK OF CARDS
SANDWICHES AND THE BEER
COME IN BOYS
EVERYTHING'S READY
©1967 Dobs + Barry Appleby
6-12

IT'S AGES SINCE YOU TOOK ME TO A DANCE
CLOAKS
ANNUAL RE·UNION DANCE
©1968
Dobs + Barry Appleby

I'M DYING TO TRY THE NEW FRUG
WILLY!
HULLO THERE

HOURS LATER
ENJOYING YOURSELF DEAR?
YES

BUT IT ISN'T QUITE WHAT I WAS EXPECTING
BAR
1-3

OOH, WHAT A PARTY IT WAS
©1962
Dobs + Barry Appleby

THOSE RE·UNIONS OF YOURS ALWAYS ARE

SORRY TO BE LATE FOR BREAKFAST, DEAR

THIS IS LUNCH
10-2

GAYE LOVES KNITTING, SHE FINDS IT SO RELAXING AND IT DOESN'T INTERFERE WITH CONVERSATION— BUT THE RESULT DOESN'T ALWAYS TURN OUT WHAT SHE EXPECTS

IT'S FINISHED
©1968
Dobs +
Barry Appleby
KNIT

TRY IT ON

TAKE ANOTHER LOOK AT THE PATTERN, DEAR
PATTERN
22-2

OH NO, NOT ANOTHER
©1968
Dobs +
Barry Appleby
KNIT

DON'T YOU LIKE ME KNITTING THINGS FOR YOU?

IT ISN'T THAT DARLING

IT'S JUST THAT I THINK YOU SPOIL ME TOO MUCH
27-2

THERE'S NOTHING QUITE SO SQUELCHING, AFTER A HARD DAY'S WORK, AS TO ARRIVE HOME ALL EAGERLY LOOKING FORWARD TO A NICE WELCOMING WIFE AND A HOT MEAL ONLY TO FIND A NOTE AND A PILE OF SANDWICHES — — GEORGE HATES IT.

©1967
Dobs+
Barry
Appleby

GEORGE, DEAR, I'LL BE A BIT LATE HOME

SO HAVE A SNACK UNTIL I GET BACK

I'VE LEFT EVERYTHING READY FOR YOU
YES
NO
9-10

COOEE, I'M HOME ... OH.. GAYE'S OUT
©1968
Dobs+Barry Appleby

I WONDER IF THAT SHOULD BE TURNED OFF ?

OR LEFT TO COOK ?

I'LL BE A LITTLE LATE HOME, DEAR
28·6

PHEW! WHAT A STORM
©1968 Dobs + Barry Appleby

I'M GLAD I HAVEN'T GOT TO GO OUT AGAIN TONIGHT

COOEE— I'M HOME

MEET ME AT—
XXX
26-2

GEORGE, I'M STILL IN TOWN WAITING FOR YOU
YOU ARE?
©1967 Dobs + Barry Appleby

YOU'RE SUPPOSED TO MEET ME WITH THE CAR
I AM?

DIDN'T YOU FIND MY NOTE WHEN YOU GOT HOME?
YES

BUT I HAVEN'T FINISHED READING IT YET
13-10

HAVE YOU NOTICED HOW MOST WOMEN FORGET THE DETAILS AND DATES OF MOST IMPORTANT INCIDENTS AND YET REMEMBER WHAT THEY AND ALL THE OTHER WOMEN WERE WEARING EVEN YEARS AFTERWARDS

FROM OUR CAREFULLY INDEXED FILES
OF THE BIGGER CARTOONS WE HAVE CHOSEN
THE DRAWINGS WHICH APPEAR ON THE
FOLLOWING PAGES

© 1967
Dobs + Barry Appleby

355

© 1967
Dobs + Barry
Appleby
EEK! — IT'S MRS BIGWEED
SPORT

AND JUST LOOK AT THE STATE OF THIS ROOM
SPORT
SEW

TIDY IT UP WHILE I KEEP HER TALKING IN THE HALL

WHERE SHALL I PUT THEM?

UNDER THE CHAIR CUSHIONS

AH MRS BIGWEED — HOW NICE TO SEE YOU

DO TAKE A SEAT

356

The Gambols
George, we really MUST have some new curtains
©1968
Dobs + Barry
Appleby

Three feet plus two feet three plus six inches for a heading

Look dear
Soft Furn
SALE ~ CURTAIN MATERIAL

How about this red velvet
Bang on

This is really LOVELY material

IDEA

365

CINDI!
GAYE DAHLING
©1968 Dobs +
Barry Appleby

HOW LOVELY TO SEE YOU

I'VE BEEN MEANING TO CALL YOU ALL WEEK...

LATER
...WELL, I WASN'T GOING TO LET HER GET AWAY WITH THAT...

EVEN LATER

389

OOH, I FEEL WORN OUT—ALL THOSE PEOPLE IN THE SHOPS—PUSHING AND SHOVING
©1968
Bobs + Barry Appleby

WELL, YOU JUST SIT DOWN AND LET ME GET THE SUPPER
SOUNDS LOVELY

COME AND GET IT
YOU ARE SWEET

WHAT ARE YOU GIVING ME?
SPAGHETTI BOLOGNAISE

ER.. WELL IF I MAY MAKE A SUGGESTION DEAR

IT NEEDS COOKING A LITTLE LONGER
388

YOU'LL BE LATE FOR CHURCH
I'M NOT COMING TO-DAY—I'M TIRED
VERY WELL, IF YOU WON'T COME WITH ME I'LL GO ON MY OWN
I WONDER IF THE PAPER'S ARRIVED
© 1968 Dobs + Barry Appleby
SLAM
382

AN EXTRA PLACE FOR SUPPER?
YES
©1968
Bobst
Barry Appleby

AGATHA 'PHONED TO-DAY AND I ASKED HER TO VISIT US
WHO'S AGATHA?

AN OLD FRIEND — I HAVEN'T SEEN HER SINCE WE WERE AT SCHOOL TOGETHER

SHE'S A NICE TIMID LITTLE MOUSE WITH 30-30-30 STATISTICS

FAILED ALL HER EXAMS AND ALWAYS BOTTOM OF THE CLASS

SHE WORE STEEL-RIMMED PEBBLE GLASSES AND SHE HADN'T A CLUE ABOUT CLOTHES

POOR GIRL — I'VE OFTEN WONDERED HOW LIFE'S BEEN TREATING HER
WELL, YOU'LL SOON KNOW

.. SHE'S JUST ARRIVING
381

THE NORTHERN IRELAND TOURIST BOARD SPENT £2,500 ON A TOURIST SURVEY AND FOUND THAT IT'S IDEAL VISITOR SHOULD BE JUST LIKE GEORGE AND GAYE GAMBOL

FISHING
BOATS FOR HIRE
FRESH BAIT
© 1968 Dobs + Barry Appleby

JUST LOOK AT THE SEA

IT'S LIKE A MILL-POND

NOT A BITE ALL MORNING

ZZZZZZZ

ZZZZZZZ

IT SEEMS A SHAME TO WAKE HIM
ZZZZZZZ

391

GEORGE, DEAR..
©1968
Dobs +
Barry Appleby

WILL YOU EMPTY THE BAG OF THE CARPET CLEANER FOR ME?
OH, VERY WELL

GEORGE!

NOT IN THE KITCHEN!

JUST LOOK AT ALL THE DUST

OH! CAN'T YOU EVEN DO A SIMPLE JOB LIKE THAT?

THAT'S THE LAST TIME I EVER ASK YOU TO EMPTY THE CLEANER

380

©1967 Bobs + Barry Appleby
GEORGE, I'M GOING TO THE HAIRDRESSER

WILL YOU MEET ME OUTSIDE AND THEN WE CAN GO HOME TOGETHER
SURE

Hairdresser

GOING TO BE LONG?

AT LEAST ANOTHER HALF-AN-HOUR

WELL, CAN I COME IN AND GET DRY?

347

WHAT'S THE MATTER, DEAR?
I'VE GOT A HEADACHE
© 1968 Dobs + Barry Appleby

WELL, STAY IN BED AND I'LL BRING YOUR BREAKFAST

BANG
THAT WAS THE KITCHEN DOOR

THUD!

CRASH
THERE GOES A PLATE

SNIFF SNIFF

MY HEADACHE'S TOO BAD FOR ME TO STAY IN BED
376

LAST WEEK
Hatique
EASTER HATS EXCLUSIVE FROM PARIS
SALE
© 1968 Dobs & Barry Appleby

HULLO MR TROWEL... AND MR SPADE
HULLO THERE

THAT'S A SMASHING HAT MRS GAMBOL
IS IT NEW?

YES, SHE'S JUST BOUGHT IT AT THE NEW HATIQUE

A REAL BARGAIN

TODAY HERE'S OLD TROWEL'S WIFE... AND MRS SPADE

YOU AND YOUR BIG MOUTH

375

The Gambols
© 1968
Dobs + Barry Appleby

CRASH

EEK

IT'S ONLY ME, DEAR

WHAT ARE YOU DOING?

GETTING A DRINK

WHY DIDN'T YOU SWITCH ON THE LIGHT?

I DIDN'T WANT TO WAKE YOU

374

HEY! WHAT ARE YOU DOING?
CLEARING OUT THE CUPBOARD
© 1968
Bobs + Barry Appleby

WELL, WELL, OUR HOLIDAY SNAPS

AND MY FOREIGN STAMPS — DON'T YOU DARE THROW THESE AWAY
STAMPS

I'LL SORT THEM OUT AND STICK THEM INTO ALBUMS
STAMPS

AND THESE RECIPES NEED FILING
PUT THEM ON THE TABLE

NOW DON'T TOUCH ANY- -THING — I'LL CARRY ON WITH THE JOB TOMORROW
1967

...AND SO EVERY EVENING
1967
1966

I'LL BE JOLLY GLAD WHEN YOU'VE FINISHED WITH THE TABLE

373

I'M GOING TO VISIT MILLY IN HOSPITAL
WHERE'S CLOUDBANK ROAD?
©1968
Dobs +
Barry
Appleby

AT THE TOP OF RACK HILL
WHERE'S THAT?

FIRST LEFT AT THE ROUNDABOUT PAST ELDERBERRY ROAD — THEN THIRD LEFT

AND SECOND... NO THIRD LEFT — THEN FIRST RIGHT

AND SECOND LEFT AND IT'S STRAIGHT AHEAD

ER.. LEFT
NO, NO, THE OTHER HAND

HERE — LET ME HELP YOU

RIGHT
LEFT

372

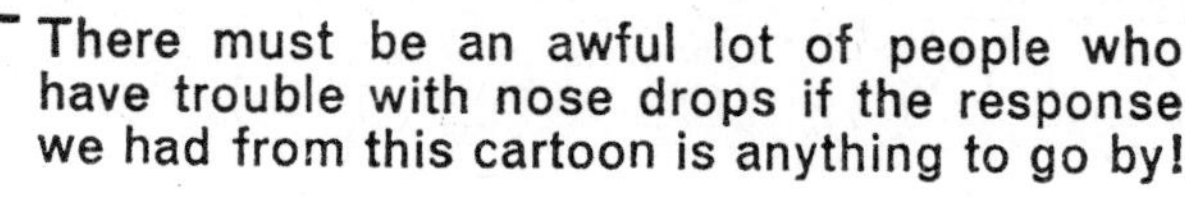

There must be an awful lot of people who have trouble with nose drops if the response we had from this cartoon is anything to go by!

387

DOTTY WANTS US TO GO TO HER PARTY
OH NO NOT ME
©1968 Bob + Barry Appleby

BUT I CAN'T REFUSE
GO ON YOUR OWN

DON'T BE SILLY— YOU MUST COME WITH ME
HER PARTIES ARE SUCH A BORE

YOU NEVER WANT TO VISIT ANY OF MY FRIENDS

WILL YOU COME — JUST TO PLEASE ME?

WE NEEDN'T STAY VERY LONG
OH, VERY WELL THEN

NOW DON'T FORGET —WE LEAVE NOT A MINUTE LATER THAN TEN O'CLOCK

MIDNIGHT
YOU ALWAYS WANT TO LEAVE WHEN I'M ENJOYING MYSELF

371

THE RECORD PLAYER'S PACKED UP
AGAIN?

IT'S WORN OUT — WE'LL HAVE TO BUY ANOTHER
WHAT WITH?

ER... I COULD SAVE MONEY WITH A SELF ASSEMBLY KIT

HERE'S ONE — "RECORD PLAYERS — MADE BY WORLD FAMOUS LONG ESTABLISHED COMPANY"
RADIO MAG

"ONLY TWO PARTS TO ASSEMBLE — REJECT EXPORT ORDER — OBSOLETE MODEL BUT IN PERFECT ORDER — SAVE POUNDS — ONLY A FEW LEFT"

GAYE, IT'S COME
THIS SIDE UP

WELL, OPEN IT THEN AND LET'S SEE IT

368

EEK! MIND THAT OIL
©1968 Dobs +
Barry Appleby

YOU'VE RUINED MY NEW DRESS
DON'T WORRY — I'LL PAY TO HAVE IT CLEANED

I'LL NEED THE SPECIAL SERVICE
HUH?

AN EXTRA TWELVE & SIX FOR HAND CLEANING
THAT'S RIDICULOUS

HARDWARE
THE WUND·DA SPOT EXTRACTOR
NEW! AMAZING IT'S A MIRACLE

THIS IS ONE WAY WE CAN SAVE MONEY

HAS THE SPOT COME OUT?

YES, DEAR
367

© 1968
Dobs + Barry Appleby
I'D LOVE A NIGHT OUT
WE CAN'T AFFORD IT

IDEA

GEORGE LET'S SAVE ALL OUR HALF-PENNIES FOR MAD MONEY
HUH?

THEN WE CAN HAVE A NIGHT OUT WITHOUT MAKING OURSELVES HARD-UP

MUCH LATER
OOH, I FEEL FED UP
WELL, LET'S SPEND OUR MAD MONEY ON A NIGHT OUT

ARE YOU READY DEAR?
JUST COMING

HAVE YOU GOT THE MONEY?

YES DEAR

363

OOOH! OF ALL THE TWO-FACED ... OOH! — AFTER ALL THE TALES SHE TOLD POLLY ABOUT ME
WELL, WRITE AND SAY YOU CAN'T GO
INVITATION
SPORT
©1967 Bob & Barry Appleby

YOU CAN'T CALL HER THAT IN WRITING

MADAM, YOU ARE A

DEAR MADAM, IF YOU THINK THAT I WOULD

DEAR MRS LILYPOOL, YOU MUST BE BONKERS IF YOU THINK

DEAR SALLY, I AM AFRAID THAT....

MY DEAREST SALLY, I WOULD LOVE TO COME BUT...

DARLING, I'D ADORE TO COME TO YOUR PARTY BUT GEORGE IS TAKING ME OUT THAT EVENING
358

RINGG
© 1967
Dobs +
Barry
Appleby
NOW WHO CAN THAT BE?
PAINT

EEK! IT'S MRS GRANDIFLORA

GEORGE! OPEN THE DOOR AND ASK HER IN

SHOW HER INTO THE SITTING ROOM
PAINT

AND ENTERTAIN HER FOR A FEW MINUTES

JUST LONG ENOUGH FOR ME TO RUSH UPSTAIRS AND CHANGE
PAINT

NO, ON SECOND THOUGHTS

GO AND HIDE
353
PAINT

WHAT'S THAT?
A NEW DRESS FOR TONIGHT'S PARTY
©1967
Dobs + Barry Appleby

SEND IT BACK — YOU DON'T NEED A NEW DRESS
BUT I HAVEN'T A THING TO WEAR

DON'T BE SILLY — I AM NOT BUYING YOU A NEW DRESS

BUT I TELL YOU I HAVEN'T A THING TO WEAR

OUR GUESTS WILL BE HERE IN A MINUTE

ARE YOU READY DEAR?
YES COMING — RIGHT AWAY

!

ALRIGHT — YOU'VE MADE YOUR POINT

GEORGE, WHAT ABOUT THAT LITTLE JOB YOU PROMISED TO DO FOR ME
I'M TOO TIRED
© 1967
Dobs + Barry Appleby

YOU'RE ALWAYS TOO TIRED - YOU NEED SOMETHING TO LIVEN YOU UP

TIRED.. LISTLESS.. NO ENERGY.. ? THEN YOU NEED BERYVIMS

ALWAYS TIRED YOU SAY — WELL THESE VITAMINS SHOULD HELP HIM

TODAY
HULLO MRS GAMBOL, DID THE VITAMINS DO YOUR HUSBAND ANY GOOD?

OH YES, THEY WERE ABSOLUTELY SUPER — THEY MADE HIM VERY LIVELY

HE'S BEEN JUMPING ALL OVER THE PLACE

NOW HE WANTS SOMETHING TO CURE HIS BAD BACK

351

AT BREAKFAST GEORGE HAS HIS HEAD STUCK IN THE MORNING PAPER AND GAYE CAN'T GET A WORD OUT OF HIM — IN THE EVENING WHEN SHE'S BURSTING WITH THE DAY'S NEWS HE AGAIN HAS HIS HEAD STUCK IN HIS NEWSPAPER.

THE MORNING PAPER HASN'T ARRIVED
WHAT SHALL WE DO?
©1968 Dobs+ Barry Appleby

WE'LL JUST HAVE TO TALK

TALK?.....AT BREAKFAST?

I'VE FORGOTTEN HOW TO
23-2

SPORT
©1968 Dobs+Barry Appleby

IT'S LOVELY WHEN YOU'RE CHEERFUL
SPORT

HUH?
SPORT

YOU HAVEN'T GRUMBLED ABOUT A SINGLE THING IN THE PAPER THIS MORNING
SPORT
10-4

MURIEL CAME IN TO BORROW SOME FLOUR AND STAYED TO TEA
©1968
Bobs+Barry Appleby

THEN THE MAN CAME TO REPAIR THE FRIDGE AND THE MILK WENT SOUR

NOW HAND ME THE PAPER

AND TELL ME ABOUT YOUR DAY
22-7

OH — FOR HEAVEN'S SAKE! — STOP CHATTERING
©1968 Bobs+Barry Appleby

CAN'T YOU SEE THAT I'M TRYING TO READ MY PAPER ?

WELL, I HAVE ONLY ONE MORE THING TO TELL YOU, DEAR
WHAT'S THAT ?

YOUR PAPER'S UPSIDE DOWN
28-5

GEORGE LOVES THE MINI-SKIRT FASHION — BUT NOT ON GAYE!

HOLIDAYS! WHAT A LONG TIME AGO IT ALL SEEMS

MOTORWAY EXIT FOR MUDIBAY 2 MILES
©1968 Bobs + Barry Appleby

MOTORWAY EXIT FOR MUDIBAY 1 MILE

MUDIBAY
MAP

PROMISE YOU WON'T SPOIL THE HOLIDAY BY GETTING CROSS ON THE VERY FIRST DAY
NEXT EXIT 12 MILES
29-7

WE'VE GIVEN YOU A LOVELY ROOM
27
©1968 Bobs + Barry Appleby

IT'S VERY QUIET

CLANG
CLONG
CLING
CLUNG

EXCEPT FOR THE CHURCH CLOCK

IT'S A BEAUTIFUL MORNING
© 1968 Dobs + Barry Appleby

RING FOR BREAKFAST DEAR

WE PAID FOR A ROOM WITH A BALCONY

SO WE MAY AS WELL HAVE BREAKFAST ON IT
31-7

WELL, SO MUCH FOR THE HORS D'OEUVRES...
© 1968 Dobs + Barry Appleby

WHAT'S NEXT?
LUNCH

THAT WAS THE LUNCH SIR...
LUNCH

...FOR THE GUESTS ON FULL PENSION TERMS
LUNCH
1-8

WHAT'S THE MATTER?
I CAN'T SLEEP

WHY NOT?

THE MATTRESS IS LUMPY

WELL, WHERE ELSE CAN WE KEEP OUR HOLIDAY MONEY?

IT'S TIME WE WENT BACK TO DINNER DEAR

THAT WAS A WONDERFUL IDEA GEORGE

WE HAD THE BAY ENTIRELY TO OURSELVES ALL DAY

THESE CHAIRS ARE NICE AND COMFY
©1968
Dobs + Barry Appleby

UNTIL YOU WANT TO GET OUT OF THEM
5-8

SHE TOLD ME THAT THEY ARE ONLY STAYING AT THE HOTEL FOR A FEW DAYS
©1968
Dobs + Barry Appleby

HER HUSBAND'S INCOME ALLOWS THEM TO HAVE SEVERAL HOLIDAYS A YEAR.. AND ONE THING LED TO ANOTHER...

BUT THAT'S WHAT I EARN IN A MONTH
I KNOW BUT.. ER..

IT SOUNDS MORE
6-8

©1968
Bobs + Barry Appleby
COME FOR A SWIM!
NO, NO, NO!

HOW WAS I TO KNOW THAT WASN'T THE SWIM-SUIT YOU SWAM IN?

I DIDN'T KNOW IT WOULD SHRINK
7-8

DON'T LET GO OF THE ROPE
©1968
Bobs + Barry Appleby

AND REMEMBER TO KEEP YOUR KNEES BENT ALL THE TIME

IT'S ALL A MATTER OF BALANCE
OF COURSE IT WILL TAKE YOU SOME TIME TO GET USED TO IT

B-8

YAWN
17
© 1968
Dobs + Barry Appleby

HURRY UP IN THE BATHROOM
WON'T BE A MINUTE DEAR

THE MAID'S LAID OUT THE WRONG PYJAMAS— THESE AREN'T MINE

WRONG ROOM
17
LIFT →
9-8

THAT YOUNG COUPLE ARE ON THEIR HONEYMOON
OH?
© 1968
Dobs + Barry Appleby

A BIT YOUNG AREN'T THEY?

WELL, YOU KNOW THE OLD SAYING —"TWO CAN LIVE AS CHEAPLY AS ONE ..."

PROVIDED SHE KEEPS HER JOB
10-8

VIEW POINT
© 1968
Dobs + Barry Appleby

16·8

STOP WORRYING ABOUT YOUR HOUSE PLANTS
© 1968
Dobs + Barry Appleby

DON'T YOU TRUST ME?

THAT INVENTION OF MINE TO WATER THEM AUTOMATICALLY WHILE WE WERE AWAY IS FOOL·PROOF

17·8

BILLS — THE CLOUD IN EVERYBODY'S LIFE

©1968 Dobs+
Barry Appleby
BILLS

WELL, THAT'S ALL THE BILLS PAID RIGHT UP TO DATE

BUT DON'T POST THEM YET

OR WE'LL BE LIVING BEYOND OUR MEANS
25-7

WE CAN'T AFFORD TO BUY IT
CATALOGUE
©1968 Dobs+ Barry Appleby

CATALOGUE
DO·IT YOURSELF

AND WE CAN'T AFFORD TO MAKE IT
DO·IT YOURSELF

THIS REALLY BRINGS HOME HOW EXPENSIVE THINGS ARE THESE DAYS
DO·IT YOURSELF
12-3

©1968 Dobst
Barry Appleby
LIGHT BILL

YOU'LL HAVE TO LEAVE MY LIGHT ON MY DRESSING TABLE

I CAN'T SEE TO PUT ON MY LIPSTICK
6-5

NOW ISN'T THIS PRETTY?
SPORT
©1968 Dobst
Barry Appleby

HUH?
SPORT

IT'S PRINTED IN A LOVELY SHADE OF RED
OH?

INSTEAD OF THAT DRAB BLACK
BANK STATEMENT
1-2

IT'S AGES SINCE I HAD A NEW DRESS
©1968 Dobs + Barry Appleby

AND THE WAY PRICES ARE RISING IS MAKING US SO HARD UP
GROCER BILL

TELL ME WHAT'S WRONG DEAR — THEN YOUR TROUBLES WON'T SEEM SO BIG

17-7

GEORGE — WE'VE OVERSLEPT
©1968 Dobs + Barry Appleby

THERE'S A HOLE IN MY SOCK

I CAN SEE THIS IS GOING TO BE ANOTHER ONE OF THOSE DAYS
SEW
5-2

F

BANG
©1968
Dobs +
Barry Appleby

GRRR
IS THAT YOU GEORGE?

THUMP

AH WELL, I DON'T NEED TO ASK WHAT SORT OF A DAY HE'S HAD
8-7

A LADDER AND MY LAST PAIR OF NYLONS
©1968
Dobs + Barry Appleby

GAYE — OUR GUEST'S CAR HAS JUST ARRIVED

THE ZIP'S BROKEN — I'LL HAVE TO WEAR MY OLD BLUE DRESS

TRY NOT TO THINK ABOUT IT DEAR
RING
14-2

THE NAME MIGGY SURPRISINGLY ENOUGH INTRIGUES SOME READERS — MIGGY IS THE NICKNAME FOR MARGARET AND THERE ARE VERY MANY HAPPY MARGARETS AROUND THE WORLD WHO ARE CALLED MIGGY BY THEIR FRIENDS

AUNTIE GAYE—YOU'LL NEVER GUESS WHAT WE'VE DONE
©1967
Dobs+
Barry Appleby

ER...NO I CAN'T GUESS

WHAT HAVE YOU DONE?

NOW LET'S GO AND TELL UNCLE GEORGE
18·8

©1967
Dobs+
Barry Appleby

GAYE! YOU'LL HURT YOURSELF SLIDING DOWN THE BANISTERS

IT'S SAFER THAN WALKING DOWN THE STAIRS, DEAR
19·8

DID I HEAR FLIVVER COME INTO THE HOUSE?
YES

WHAT DID HE WANT?
THE CAR KEY
SPORT

OH
SPORT

© 1967. Dobs + Barry Appleby
21-8

© 1967 Dobs + Barry Appleby

RING

22/8

SHE'S PUT THE CAKES IN THE TOP CUPBOARD

THAT'S SUPPOSED TO BE OUT OF OUR REACH

CLIMB ON MY SHOULDERS

ACT NONCHALANT
BISCUITS
CRACKERS
COFFEE
CHEESE
© 1967 Dobs + Barry Appleby
23-8

MORNING
© 1967
Dobs + Barry Appleby

NOON

AFTERNOON

EVENING
YOU AND YOUR "I'VE BOUGHT THEM SOMETHING TO KEEP THEM OUT OF MISCHIEF"
25-8

OOWA OOWA OOWA
I'M BIG CHIEF
SITTING BULL
© 1967
Dobs
Barry Appleby

I'VE SCALPED
MIGGY
GEORGE,
STOP HIM

DON'T WORRY, DEAR
THEY'RE ONLY PLAYING
COWBOYS AND INDIANS

BUT THAT'S MY
NEW WIG
31-8

I'M WORRIED
ABOUT MIGGY
OH? WHAT'S THE
MATTER WITH
HER?
SPORT
© 1967
Dobs + Barry Appleby

I DON'T THINK
SHE'S VERY WELL
SPORT

MIGGY, PUT OUT
YOUR TONGUE
DEAR

IT IS OUT
4-9

NO, YOU CAN'T HAVE ANOTHER ICE — YOU'VE HAD TWO ALREADY
MARKET
©1967 Dobs+Barry Appleby

LET'S GET LOST

POLICE
WE'RE LOST

IT WORKS EVERY TIME
5-9

GO AWAY
©1967
Dobs+Barry Appleby

OH LET HER STAY AND WATCH YOU, DEAR

SHE MAKES ME NERVOUS
OH? WHY?

SHE'S WAITING FOR ME TO BURN MYSELF
6-9

© 1967
Dobs + Barry Appleby

8-9

© 1967 Dobs + Barry Appleby

9-9

CAN I CUT MYSELF A PIECE OF CAKE?
© 1967 Dobs + Barry Appleby

YES, DEAR

CAN I CUT MIGGY SOME TOO?
YES DEAR

17-8

TRY THE ONE IN THE HIGH STREET
© 1968 Dobs + Barry Appleby

NO?... WELL THANK YOU ANYWAY

HE WON'T TAKE HER EITHER

WELL, THERE MUST BE A DENTIST SOMEWHERE THAT SHE HASN'T BITTEN
TELEPHONE DIRECTORY
15-1

©1968
Dobs +
Barry Appleby
SOMETIMES I JUST DON'T WANT TO GROW UP— NOT EVER
BILL
1-1

DID YOU CATCH FLIVVER?
NO, HE GOT AWAY WHEN I GRABBED HIM
©1967
Dobs +
Barry Appleby
BUT DONT WORRY— HE'LL SOON BE BACK
HOW DO YOU KNOW?
14.9

©1967
Dobs +
Barry
Appleby

WELL.. ER.. IT'S RATHER A LONG STORY
15-9

HERE'S THE MONEY
HAIRDRESSER
BOYS HALF PRICE
©1968 Dobs + Barry Appleby

AND YOU GO WITH HIM MIGGY — AND MAKE SURE THAT HE GETS HIS HAIR CUT

HAIRDRESSER
BOYS HALF PRICE

NOW NONE OF THE FELLOWS WILL KNOW THAT I PLAY WITH A GIRL
HAIRDR
16-1

© 1968 Dobs & Barry Appleby

A PEARL!

GAYE — WE'RE RICH

DARLING! YOU'VE FOUND MY EARRING
12-8

RING BELL IN CASE OF EMERGENCY ONLY
© 1968 Dobs + Barry Appleby

NO. NO. GAYE
RING IN C EMER ONL

BUT I'VE GOT A LADDER IN MY STOCKING

AND IF THAT ISN'T AN EMERGENCY I DON'T KNOW WHAT IS
RIN IN EM ON
13-8

8 P.M.
I'LL SIT AND WATCH YOU DEAR
HOTEL BILLIARD COMPETITION
© 1968 Dobs + Barry Appleby

9 P.M.

10·30 P.M.
BRAVO, GEORGE, YOU'RE IN THE QUARTER-FINAL

MIDNIGHT
I'M AFRAID I'M NOT VERY GOOD COMPANY FOR YOU TO-NIGHT DEAR
14·8

© 1968 Dobs + Barry Appleby

LOOK, I KNOW I NEGLECTED YOU LAST EVENING

AND I KNOW THAT YOU'RE CROSS WITH ME

BUT STOP INTRODUCING ME AS YOUR FIRST HUSBAND
15·8

THERE'S ONE WE COULD AFFORD TO PAY CASH FOR
Used Cars
GOOD RUNNER
© 1967 Dobs + Barry Appleby

TRY IT OUT YOURSELF— BUT WATCH—THE BRAKES ARE A BIT DODGY

AH, WELL BACK TO THE CARS WE CAN NOT AFFORD TO PAY CASH FOR
28/11

SO YOU'VE FINALLY MADE UP YOUR MIND
YES
© 1967 Dobs + Barry Appleby

AND WE ARE NOW THE PROUD OWNERS OF A NEW CAR?

I'VE JUST POSTED THE CHEQUE

GOODBYE FUR COAT
8-12

THE WORLD IS DIVIDED INTO TWO KINDS OF WOMAN—
-THE ONES WHO LIKE TO TAKE THEIR HUSBANDS WITH
THEM WHEN THEY GO SHOPPING AND THE OTHERS WHO
WOULDN'T LET THEIR HUSBANDS ACCOMPANY THEM
UNDER **ANY** CIRCUMSTANCES .... BUT WITHOUT
EXCEPTION ALL SHOP ASSISTANTS **HATE** GEORGE
TO BE PRESENT WHEN GAYE BUYS A DRESS

BUT IN SPITE OF ALL THE BILLS WE
JUST HAD TO FIND THE MONEY FOR
A NEW CAR

JUST WHY MUST WE BUY A NEW CAR?
CARS FOR SALE
© 1967
Dobs + Barry Appleby

BECAUSE THIS ONE USES TOO MUCH PETROL AND WE MUST ECONOMISE

SO WE'RE SPENDING HUNDREDS OF POUNDS TO SAVE A TINY DROP OF PETROL
ER...YES

WELL, IF I USED THAT ARGUMENT YOU'D SAY I WAS BONKERS
24-11

CAREFULLY MAINTAINED
Used Cars
© 1967 Dobs + Barry Appleby

LOW MILEAGE

ONE OWNER— A VERY CAREFUL DRIVER

NEVER EXCEEDED 25 MILES AN HOUR
30-11

© 1967
Dobs + Barry Appleby

22-9

© 1967
Dobs + Barry Appleby

26-9

BAD DAYS — GOOD DAYS — RED DAYS
BLUE DAYS — JOLLY DAYS — GLOOMY
DAYS — HAPPY DAYS — DISMAL DAYS —
ONE OF THOSE DAYS — WE ALL HAVE THEM

Love from Gaye
Love from George
WHEN DO YOU OPEN YOUR CHRISTMAS PRESENTS? GEORGE AND GAYE OPEN THEIR'S AS SOON AS THEY WAKE — JUST LIKE CHILDREN

OOH—WHAT A THING TO SAY —WHAT A HORRIBLE WOMAN I WON'T TAKE THIS LYING DOWN
© 1967 Dobs + Barry Appleby

I'LL WRITE HER A LETTER

YOU CAN'T POST THIS— IT'LL LAND YOU IN ALL SORTS OF TROUBLE
I DON'T INTEND TO POST IT

BUT IT'S MADE ME FEEL A LOT BETTER FOR WRITING IT
18-12

© 1967 Dobs + Barry Appleby
ICING

ICI

ICI

20-12

OOH DARLING — THANK YOU — WHAT IS IT?
GUESS
Merry Christmas
©1967 Dobs + Barry Appleby

A FUR STOLE?
ER..NO
A DIAMOND RING?
ER... NO
NEGLIGEE?... HOUSECOAT?
NO

YOU WILL BE SURPRISED

I AM·
IRON
25-12

THAT'S INTERESTING
ENCYCLOPEDIA
©1967 Dobs + Barry Appleby

GAYE, DID YOU KNOW THAT GRASS IS AN IMPORTANT ORDER OF MONOCOTYLEDONS AND THERE ARE ABOUT 4,500 SPECIES?
ENCYCLOPEDIA

GAYE...
ENCYCLOPEDIA

AREN'T YOU INTERESTED?
26-12

AND THAT'S ALL WE HAVE ROOM FOR — BUT
DON'T FORGET WE'LL BE SEEING YOU IN THE
MORNING — SAME TIME — SAME PLACE

George
& Gaye